If Frogs Made Weather

by Marion Dane Bauer

illustrated by Dorothy Donohue

Holiday House/New York

Library of Congress Cataloging-in-Publication Data

Bauer, Marion Dane.
If frogs made weather / written by Marion Dane
Bauer; illustrated by Dorothy Donohue. — 1st ed.

p. cm.

Summary: A young child ruminates on the
favorite weather of ten different animals.

ISBN 0-8234-1622-4

1. Animals — Juvenile fiction.
[1. Animals — Fiction. 2. Weather — Fiction.]
I. Donohue, Dorothy, ill. II. Title.

PZ10.3.B317If 2005

[E] — dc22

2003064729

Designed by Yvette Lenhart

To Kyra
M. D. B.

To My Magnificent Seven,
Lily, Nathan, Sam, Ashton, Jaden,
Spencer, and especially Hunter
D. D.

If frogs made weather,
morning would sprinkle.
Afternoon would drip.
Night would whisper,
whisper to the brimming ponds,
"Did you know that frogs
make weather?"

If weasels made weather,
fog would cling to the ground,
grip the grass.

If weasels made weather,
mist would hide the slink,
conceal the pounce.

Breakfast!

If robins made weather,
trees would always be budding,
the grass fresh and green.
And the melting snow
would set every worm awiggling.

If cats made weather, sun would slant
in every window, spy beneath each bush,
warm a spot for a tight-tucked nap,
warm a spot for a *s-t-r-e-t-c-h*.

If flies made weather,
every day would be hot, **hot**, **hot**.
All the food would rot, **rot**, **rot**.
And every fly would buzz.

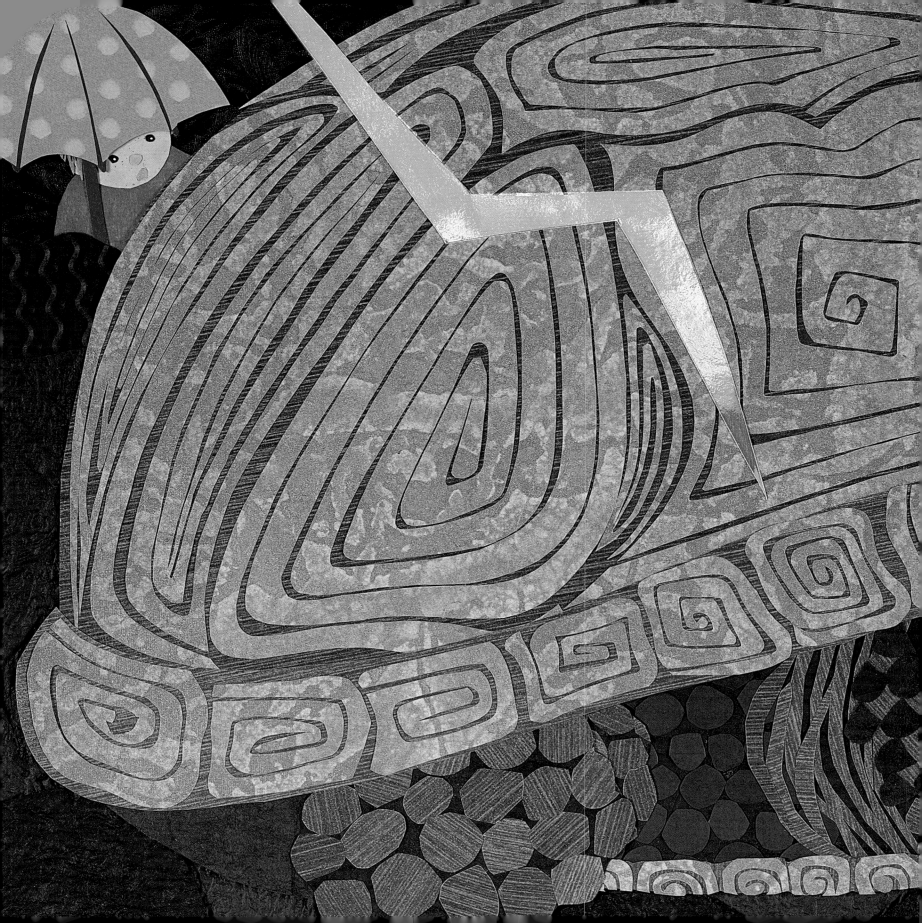

If turtles made weather,
lightning would crash
and smash and sizzle.
Turtles would snap their
doors shut and smile
in the dry dark.

If bats made weather,
the sun would sink,
the wind would still.

Every mosquito
would hum its fill.

And all the bats
would be full of
mosquitoes.

If hawks made weather,
the wind would blow and **blow**,
rising and **rising**,
swirling and **swirling**.
Hawks would stretch
their wings
and drift,
drift
down.

If geese made weather,
leaves would flare
in the bright blue air.
Frost would tip the lawn.
And the sky would sigh
with the lonely cry of
"Going. Going. Gone."

If polar bears made weather,
snow would pelt.
Snow would sting.
Snow would pile
and drift and cling.
If polar bears made weather,
we would never see spring!

If I made weather, I would call
the slanting sun to my bed.
I would tiptoe through the fog.
I would blow the day clear
with a mighty wind.

I would leave my footprints
in the damp new earth
and twirl the leaves to their beds.
I would bask in heat
and rejoice in snow.

I would snuggle in my mama's lap
to hear the lightning roar.
And I would stay,
counting the drip, **drip**, **drip**.

When the sun slid
down the sky,
I would greet
the sweet nightfall.

If I made weather,
we would have it all.